conran

DESIGN

guides

Series Editor Joanna Bradshaw
Editor Mary Davies
Editorial Assistant Sally Poole
Design Paul Welti
Illustrator Cherrill Parris
Picture Research Nadine Bazar
Picture Research
Assistant Gareth Jones
Production Sonya Sibbons

First published in 1990 by
Conran Octopus Limited
37 Shelton Street,
London WC2H 9HN

Text copyright © 1990 Jeremy
Myerson and Sylvia Katz

British Library Cataloguing in
Publication Data
Myerson, Jeremy
  Kitchenware
  1. Household kitchen
equipment, history
  I. Title II. Katz, Sylvia 1944-
  III. Series
  683.8

ISBN 1-85029-262-0

Typeset by
Servis Filmsetting Limited
Printed by Wing King Tong

ACKNOWLEDGMENTS

The publisher thanks the following
photographers and organizations
for their kind permission to
reproduce the photographs in this
book:
5 above centre Bodum; 6 Mary
Evans Picture Library; 7
Reproduced by permission of the
Trustees of the Science Museum; 9
Mary Evans Picture Library; 16 left
DP Milan; 16 right Archivio Gio
Ponti; 24 left Conran Design
Group; 24 right Henning
Christoph; 25 above courtesy
Design Museum; 25 below Henning
Christoph; 26 left Reproduced by
permission of the Trustees of the
Science Museum; 27 left Siemens –
Museum; 28 Braun AG; 29 above
Braun AG; 30 below courtesy
Design Museum; 31 Pentagram; 32
above Braun AG; 32 below La
Maison de Marie Claire (Primois/
Pellé); 33 below Magimix; 34–35
Bodum; 36 Conran Design Group;
37 Henry Dreyfuss Associates; 38
Kartell; 39–39 Roger Haywood
Associates; 39 DP Milan; 40 above
Clive Corless/Conran Octopus; 40
below David Mellor; 41 left Mike
O'Neill Associates; 42 below
Hammarplast; 43 Nick Holland
Design Group; 44 left EKS Ltd;
44–45 Forma House Ltd; 45 right
Bodum; 48 above Conran Design
Group; 48–49 Henning Christoph;
49 By Courtesy of the Board of
Trustees of the Victoria and Albert
Museum; 50 Rosti Housewares; 51
above Aldo Ballo; 51 below
courtesy Design Museum; 52
courtesy Design Museum; 53 below
Conran Design Group; 54
Seymour Powell; 55 above DP
Milan; 55 below Castle Brown
Company; 58 above Reproduced
by Permission of the Trustees of
the Science Museum; 58 below
Angelo Hornak © DACS, London
1990; 59 Henning Christoph; 60
Bodum; 61 left Aldo Ballo; 61 right
Gaggia SpA.; 62 left Henning
Christoph; 62 right Clive Corless/
Conran Octopus; 63 left courtesy
Design Museum; 63 right Cona
Coffee Machine Company; 64 above
Katz collection; 64 below Studio
Nurmesniemi; 65 above Katz
collection; 65 below Conran
Design Group; 66 Aldo Ballo; 67
DP Milan; 68 left Krups; 68 right
DP Milan; 69 left David Mellor; 69
right Philips Electronics; 70 EMSA
(UK) Ltd; 73 Henry Dreyfuss
Associates; 75 Pentagram; 77–78
DP Milano.

The following photographs were
taken specially for Conran
Octopus by Simon Lee:

2–3, 5 top, below and bottom, 17,
22–23, 26 right, 27 right, 29 below,
30 above, 31 below, 33 above, 34–
35, 41 right, 42 above, 46–47, 53
above, 56–57, 71.

We would like to thank the
following for their cooperation:
Patrick Cook
ICTC (for Cuisinox and Hallen)
Design Museum
Forma House Ltd
Magimix
David Mellor
Polly Powell

Every effort has been made to
trace the copyright holders and we
apologize in advance for any
unintentional omission and would
be pleased to insert the
appropriate acknowledgment in
any subsequent edition of this
publication.

**AUTHORS'
ACKNOWLEDGMENTS**
The authors wish to thank all
those manufacturers and designers
who answered queries and
searched through their archives,
the supportive and professional
staff at Conran Octopus and Sir
Terence Conran for his personal
interest and guidance.

NOTE TO READER
Names of objects and designers
printed in roman or **bold** type
denote that a photograph of the
object or a biography of the
designer can be found elsewhere in
the book.

INTRODUCTION 6

1:MACHINES AND
APPLIANCES 23

2:UTENSILS AND
GADGETS 35

3:POTS AND
PANS 47

4:KETTLES AND
COFFEEPOTS 57

BIOGRAPHIES 72

INDEX 80

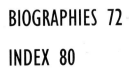

THE SPECIALIZED WORLD OF THE KITCHEN

Ever since archaeologists found a frying pan amid the ruins of Pompeii, the utensils and gadgets that people have used to prepare food have been an important measure of how far society has progressed.

Today's kitchen equipment has a lineage stretching back in time to Jericho 4000 years BC, the earliest recorded use of cooking utensils. The Romans made daily use of kettles, pots, sieves, knives and spoons, and in many cases our modern-day equivalents have not been much updated. Techniques and tools from Roman times – for example, their bronze and metal colanders (colare is the Latin word for 'to strain') – have remained part of our batterie de cuisine throughout the twentieth century.

But while some traditional concepts have endured, this century has also produced a series of dramatic technological breakthroughs which have radically transformed the kitchen and the equipment used in it. New materials such as heat-resistant glass, stainless steel and high-performance plastics have reshaped existing functions and created new ones; the advent of mass-production techniques and domestic electricity has revolutionized life in the home, making domestic appliances more convenient, varied and available.

Running in the slipstream of this scientific and technological advance has been a century of far-reaching design innovation, taking as its cue profound social, cultural, artistic and economic change in Europe, North America and the Far East. But design expression in kitchenware has been most closely linked to function, to the ability of the blade or measuring bowl to match and assist the human hand and eye in the labour-intensive business of preparing food. It is only within the past decade that designers have begun to explore the broader symbolism of, say, coffeepots or kettles as an exercise in style.

French kitchen, 1855: food-preparation techniques are a sure measure of social progress.

With a few notable exceptions, the master architects and designers of the modern age have hesitated at the door of the kitchen – as though it were a private, specialized world not worthy of a display of their talents. Significantly, objects which are taken to the dining table are treated differently to those which never venture over the kitchen threshold.

But the noted absence from the kitchen of some of the legendary names of modern design has in no way hampered the production of beautiful and practical classics in kitchenware during this century. On the contrary, such is the specialized nature of kitchen equipment that many of the most satisfying products have emerged from kitchenware manufacturing companies specifically set up to exploit a particular skill. The French company Sabatier, whose kitchen knives have a professional quality and precision dating back to the 1880s, falls into this category.

The designers involved in these companies are less familiar to us and in many cases unknown; they are often company owners or employees rather than consultants; and sometimes even chemists and engineers rather than trained designers. But their abilities are not in doubt.

Professional industrial designers have, however, paid more attention to kitchen products as the century has progressed.

Labour-intensive Victorian kitchen: cheap labour could be relied on to do the work.

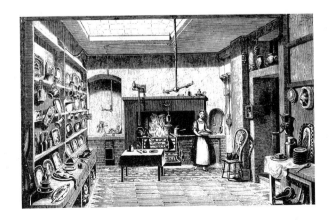

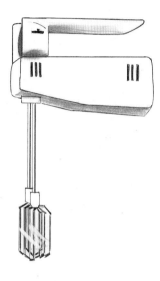

Braun hand-mixer, 1960: large manufacturers brought corporate design into the kitchen.

Kitchenware became increasingly mechanized and electrical in the years after World War Two and the bigger multinational companies – each with a design ethos broadly defined in other production sectors, such as radios and shavers began to take a keen interest in the kitchen. The German company Braun AG, founded in 1921, exemplified this trend.

More recently, within the past decade, the kitchen has reclaimed the status it had in the nineteenth century and earlier times as the hub of domestic life, in many ways the most important room in the house (and the most complex). That has concentrated fresh attention on the objects in it, leading to a further wave of design activity as the hidden appliances of food and drink preparation come into a more public domain.

This book, in choosing some 70 classics of kitchen equipment, charts the relationship designers have had with the kitchen during the twentieth century, and examines the changes in culinary trends and codes of living which are implicit in the selection.

THE MODERN INDUSTRIAL AGE

In a sense, the development of modern kitchenware began during the Industrial Revolution in England. The change from an agrarian to an urban economy inevitably brought about a major transformation in cooking and eating habits. The first cast-iron gas-stoves appeared in London in 1841 and the catalogue of the Great Exhibition of 1851 reveals an entire kitchen range on display.

The kitchens of Victorian and Edwardian England were highly labour-intensive places as a large, hierarchical domestic staff scurried about below stairs in the houses of the prosperous. An abundance of kitchen gadgets proliferated as there were always hands to do the work. It was only in the years after World War One that the focus in the kitchen switched from being labour intensive to labour saving. Two factors

Nineteenth-century kitchen tools: gadgets proliferated before labour-saving became the focus.

LA CUISINE.

brought this about. First, domestic servants went into the factories to gain more money and independence. Second, the Modern movement in design encouraged the mass production of more accessible, inexpensive, well-made objects.

The Bauhaus, the German design school which opened in 1919 under the direction of the architect Walter Gropius, was the source of Modernism. The ideological aim of its founders was to establish the Functionalist design ethic as the language of mass production; the school has had an effect on international design which has far outweighed its size and longevity. Among its students, designers such as the German Wilhelm Wagenfeld went on to devote a lifetime to producing pure utilitarian objects for the home, including, for example, a series of modular glass storage-jars.

Peter Behrens, who became artistic adviser to the giant German industrial company AEG in 1907, was influential in the Bauhaus movement. Behrens had employed Walter Gropius as a design assistant and set about formulating a coherent, modern design policy which he applied to all of AEG's products, exhibitions, buildings and printed material. His designs for a variety of utilitarian objects – from fans to lamps – did much to promote an undecorated, functional style. In particular the elegant simplicity of his nickel-plated steel electric kettle of 1908 is significant in the development of modern kitchenware.

The design focus switched to the USA in the 1930s as Hitler forced many of the leading lights of the Bauhaus, Walter Gropius among them, to flee across the Atlantic. At that time, a group of American industrial designers – including Raymond Loewy, Henry Dreyfuss, Walter Dorwin Teague and Norman Bel Geddes – were laying the foundations of the modern international design-consultancy business by setting up large practices in New York to service multinational clients.

Out of the Great Depression came the heyday of Machine Age design in the 1930s: streamlining and other styling devices were used to make products appealing to the American housewife. Henry Dreyfuss's 1936 range of kitchen utensils for the Washburn Company epitomizes the new consumer confidence in design.

Dreyfuss was a former stage designer whose first industrial-design exercise was to rework a traditional storage-jar. Raymond Loewy, a flamboyant Frenchman who arrived in New York in 1919 to work initially as a fashion illustrator, was another influential figure. Loewy's belief that 'la laideur se vend mal' (ugliness does not sell) won over many American industrialists. He became rich and famous on the strength of a series of major design commissions, including Coldspot kitchen refrigerators.

In the years after 1945, the modern kitchen, awash with gadgets, was second only to the tail-finned car in epitomizing the American Dream. The introduction of stainless steel and plastics realized an age of streamlined living. A clean, uniform kitchen environment had been standardized, rationalized and tailored to suit the economics of manufacturing. The origins of this uncluttered Modernist approach lay in designs by Mies van der Rohe for the Weissenhof Apartments in Stuttgart in 1927.

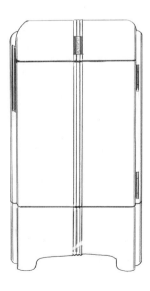

Coldspot refrigerator by Raymond Loewy for Sears Roebuck, 1935: 'Ugliness does not sell'.

Just as a home was 'a machine for living in' (Le Corbusier), so a kitchen was 'a machine for preparing meals in'.

Modernist ideals also played a part in the reconstruction of European industry after World War Two. In Britain, prototypes for the 'ideal' fitted kitchen were shown at the 1946 Britain Can Make It exhibition, designed by Milner Gray and William Vaughan. Gray had founded Britain's first industrial-design consultancy, Design Research Unit, in 1943 and he went on to design Pyrex glass ovenware in the 1950s.

Much of the impetus to improve the standard of British domestic products was centred around the Council for Industrial Design (later known as the Design Council). Under the direction of Gordon Russell, this state-funded organization opened a Design Centre in London in 1956 to promote well-designed UK-made goods including kitchenware. A year later it started its own awards scheme (known today as the British Design Awards) and in 1959 it set up a selection programme to allow chosen products to carry a seal of design approval. This scheme ran successfully for many years, enjoying international recognition. It was closed down in 1988.

Among the young British companies in the vanguard of design change was Kenwood, a maker of electric appliances. It had been founded in 1947 by a young entrepreneur called Kenneth Wood in a garage in Woking in southern England. Kenwood's first product was a toaster but a year later it produced the first all-British food mixer, and in 1950 introduced the Kenwood Chef. This milestone machine was the start of a long line of Kenwood innovations: it could perform a variety of functions with attachments converting it into a juice extractor, liquidizer, shredder, sieving machine, mincer, coffee mill, potato peeler, can opener and pulverizer. By the time the Kenwood Chef was redesigned by Kenneth Grange of Pentagram a decade later, the Kenwood name was synonymous with electrical labour-saving in the kitchen.

Kenwood's first product, the A100 Turn-Over toaster of 1947: the herald of greater things.

Italian Vitam fruit press: sculptural statement as designers elevate status of gadgets.

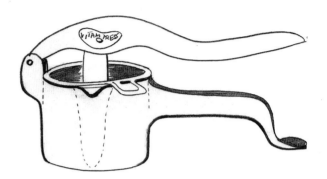

In Italy, meanwhile, the Compasso d'Oro awards were founded in 1954 by Aldo Borletti of a Milan department store, La Rinascente, to encourage designers and industrialists to strive for higher standards. Compasso d'Oro was significant because it encouraged designers working in Italy to regard mundane domestic items such as kitchen buckets and colanders as legitimate opportunities for artistic and sculptural statements. Indeed Gino Colombini's 1958 lemon squeezer for Kartell won a Compasso d'Oro in 1959, while a plastic bucket by the same manufacturer was selected for the Museum of Modern Art in New York. Designers began to emerge in Italian society as the visionaries of the future: their stylish interpretations of home products would give the nation a new status in world trade.

Germany too was picking up the pieces. Max Braun's electrical company passed to his two sons when the founder died at his desk in 1951. In 1955 Braun appointed a new chief designer, Dieter Rams, who was destined to become Europe's most important industrial designer. Together with Fritz Eichler and Hans Gugelot, Rams was responsible for creating a new design ethic for all Braun products which was enormously successful in world markets and highly influential. Braun's celebrated KM321 Kitchen Machine of 1957 is one of the most important classics of the twentieth century. A study in technical harmony, it was to remain in production for more than twenty years.

By the 1960s the design spotlight was again upon Europe. Industrial companies in the USA were large, unwieldy and introspective in their mergers and takeovers, and smaller, often family-owned European firms had taken up the design baton. That situation still exists today, with the current revival of design interest in American housewares focused on importing or interpreting European style.

In the kitchen equipment sector in particular, greater travel after 1945 led to an increased willingness to accept new cultures and an explosion of interest in new cuisines. By 1964 Terence Conran was able to open his first Habitat housewares store successfully. Five years later fellow British designer-craftsman David Mellor followed suit with the first of a series of kitchenware shops. Both of these retail ventures were significant in that for the first time professional designers with conviction and taste were making a highly personal selection of

Catalogues by David Mellor and Terence Conran's Habitat: taste was design-led from the 1960s.

items for the kitchen. Their merchandise, mixing craft products with mass-produced ones, influenced the homes of an entire generation of young, affluent consumers. Importantly, they set a pattern for kitchen equipment which reflected the way many traditional objects had survived changes in production techniques and materials technology to endure alongside more recent inventions.

THE SURVIVAL OF TRADITION

The degree to which traditional concepts in kitchenware have managed to coexist during this century alongside the results of technological change varies considerably. Some products have changed scarcely at all: others are unrecognizable.

The most ancient of all kitchen tools are the knife, the cauldron and the spit. The knife persists to this day; the cauldron has disappeared except from perhaps primitive African or South American societies; the spit has been banished from the kitchen to become the barbecue on the patio.

Pots, pans and pepper mills have an enduring functionality and any changes have been in use of materials. Hand-operated coffee grinders too have been little affected by new thinking.

Tradition and innovation: German Bakelite coffee grinder by Pieter Dienes, for PeDe 1924.

The first coffee grinder was developed in the mid-seventeenth century when coffee first arrived in Britain. It was made of lignum vitae, a hardwood, with blades of fine steel. Later, as coffee beans were roasted and ground in mills at home the coffee grinder sat on the sideboard, a decorative as well as functional object: only recently has it returned to the confines of the kitchen.

Kitchen scales emerged in the European kitchens of the eighteenth century as affluent households revelling in the introduction of fruits, sugars and spices from trade with the New World and the Far East took a far greater interest in cuisine and a more precise approach to food preparation. Scales brought science to the kitchen, and traditional metal beam-balance scales endure to this day. This is despite many design updates, for example the high-style kitchen scales designed by Marco Zanuso for the French firm Terraillon in 1973 and other ultra-sophisticated electronic varieties produced in the 1980s.

The principle of the toaster goes back to the Middle Ages when enormous fires in the middle of the room were surrounded by browning forks and revolving hooks. The first electric toaster did not appear until 1913, when General Electric in the USA launched a model which held the bread on a rack between vertical metal elements fixed to a porcelain base.

The toaster as stylistic object: streamlining trends influenced the look of a 1940s German design.

Thermostatic control was developed in the 1920s, and once that principle was established the toaster became the most conspicuous of kitchen products, prey to stylistic changes in consumer design (such as streamlining in the 1930s and 1940s) and incorporating progressively more complicated electronics (to enable, for instance, 'variable browning'). In the 1970s and 1980s the toaster lost some of its evocative decorative form, reduced in many cases to a simple white square box reflecting microchip conformity. But current revivals of toaster classics suggest new interest in the product's identity.

La Pavoni commercial espresso machine: designed by Gio Ponti for Pavoni, 1948.

Traditional Neapolitan coffeepot design: reworked by Riccardo Dalisi for Alessi in 1979.

Another contemporary revival of interest centres on the culture and technology of coffee-making. France was at the heart of the emergence of coffee-making in the late eighteenth and early nineteenth centuries, and in 1843 the first espresso machine was developed by Edward Loysel de Santais. This machine forced hot water through coffee under pressure and was a departure from the drip-pots and coffee filters that had gone before.

Italy has taken over from France as the home of innovation in the twentieth century. In Milan in 1944, for instance, Achille Gaggia patented the first espresso machine without steam and 40 years later in the same city Aldo Rossi defined the modern cafetière for design-conscious manufacturer Alessi. A reinterpretation of the traditional Neapolitan coffeepot by Riccardo Dalisi for Alessi in 1979 had triggered widespread interest in new versions of classic forms among leading architects and designers.

CHANGES IN MATERIALS TECHNOLOGY

No single factor has been more dominant in shaping the direction of modern kitchenware design than materials technology. New developments in steel, glass and plastics have resulted in some of the most significant departures of the twentieth century.

The biggest changes have been caused by the development of plastics. The first synthetic to appear in the kitchen was Bakelite, which was patented by Dr Leo Baekeland in 1907. In the 1920s it was used for colanders and egg cups but it gave off an unpleasant smell when in contact with moisture and had an unattractive mottled appearance. Bakelite was swiftly replaced by a material called urea formaldehyde, which had been developed in 1924. The Thermos flask of 1930 demonstrated the material's improved visual qualities and suitability for kitchen appliances.

There was, however, a more significant breakthrough in 1939 with the commercialization of LDPE, or low-density polyethylene, which was invented by Imperial Chemical Industries (ICI) in Britain. In 1942 an American chemist and engineer called Earl Tupper injected paraffin-like polyethylene

Bakelite for eggcups: earliest use of plastics in the kitchen but swiftly replaced by urea formaldehyde.

into moulds and so invented kitchen containers with an airtight seal which were flexible and unbreakable. Earl Tupper founded the Tupper Plastics Company in 1942, opening his first factory in Massachusetts.

Later the company supplemented polyethylene with new resins coming into commercial use. In 1956 HDPE or high-density polyethylene was introduced in West Germany: it was tougher and more heat resistant and was used for ice buckets, refrigerator linings, vacuum-cleaner housings, and so on. A year later polypropylene was developed in Italy: this could withstand boiling so machines using it as a housing could be sterilized. At last designers had a clean and hygienic covering for the new electric machines in the kitchen.

But more was to follow. In the late 1950s Dow Chemicals in the USA developed the prince of all plastics: ABS (Acrylonitrile Butadiene Styrene). ABS proved expensive but it is very tough with a high-gloss finish. It can also be metallized, providing a metal trim on, for example, food-mixer bodies. In 1958 American scientists also invented polyacetal, a material which revolutionized the kettle. This clever, practical plastic stays cool to the touch despite boiling and limescale does not stick to it. Polyacetal ushered in the era of plastics jug kettles. The pioneering Futura Forgettle electric kettle, designed in 1973 by the Russell Hobbs in-house team led by Julius Thalmann, was made of this material.

To round off an exciting decade in plastics, polycarbonate, a transparent engineering plastics, was developed in Germany in 1959. This provided a high-tech replacement for glass on those machines such as coffee-makers and food mixers which require a transparent window or body.

Polycarbonate, ABS and other plastics available by the late 1950s did much to fashion the clinical look of the modern kitchen. Plastics have been further developed to withstand the shock of short bursts of high temperatures; this has allowed the existence of the microwave. Certainly the impact of plastics in the kitchen should not be underestimated. Even the first plastics washing-up bowl, soft and unchippable, must have made a big difference after enamelled metal.

Cast-iron and tin-sheet pots and pans were a feature of the kitchens of the mid-nineteenth century. A method of coating cast iron with a layer of porcelain enamel led to improvements from 1850 onwards in Germany and Austria when enamelware emerged as an industry. Later, when more sophisticated, chemically enamelled cast-iron cookware was introduced by a company called Le Creuset in northern France in 1925, a design classic was created with a durable, resistant finish.

Aluminium, meanwhile, had been developed in the late nineteenth century. After 1910 its use was extended to kitchenware, one of the most successful examples being a series of aluminium cooking utensils designed by Lurelle Guild in 1934 for the Wear Ever company in the USA. But the most significant advance in metal kitchenware was the development of stainless steel in the 1930s.

Domestic stainless steel has 18 per cent chromium and eight per cent nickel, and was widely introduced after World War Two. Its advantages in the kitchen were quickly apparent: it was durable, clean and lightweight, and did away with the need to enamel or electro-plate metals to protect foodstuffs from contact with harmful pan surfaces.

However, stainless steel has the disadvantage of being a poor conductor of heat, and many culinary experts swiftly recommended its use in conjunction with copper, which has exceptionally good conductivity. In the USA, the Revere Copper and Brass Company's Revere Ware range of 1939, which plated copper to the base of stainless-steel cooking equipment, was a distinctive response.

But it was European designers who best exploited the aesthetic qualities of stainless steel in the years after 1945. The

1930s aluminium kettle by Lurelle Guild: the Modernist movement made a breakthrough in the USA.

Pot from the 1939 Revere Ware range designed by W Archibald Welden: stainless-steel cookware with a copper base to aid performance.

material became closely associated with the Scandinavian Modern movement, which was very popular in the USA in the 1950s and 1960s, but the outstanding kitchen product to emerge was a magnificent stainless-steel fish dish *designed by the Italian Roberto Sambonet in 1954. The Italians have explored the qualities of stainless steel, particularly its stackability, with remarkable success: the* Le Pentole *cooking system of 1979, designed by Niki Sala for the Italian company ICM, has become an international cult classic.*

Just as the development of stainless steel revolutionized metal kitchenware, so the invention of heat-resistant glass (known as Pyrex) in 1915 at the Corning glassworks in the USA radically changed the use of glassware in the kitchen. In 1827 mould pressing of glass by machine began in the USA, so bringing cheap glass onto the market for the first time, and the screw-top glass jar was patented in New York by John L Mason in 1858.

But Corning's development of Pyrex, which is made from borosilicate glass and so has a slow expansion rate and good chemical stability when heated, was a quantum leap. Although developed for the American railroad companies, it swiftly proved its worth in the kitchen – enabling vessels to be carried from oven to table. In its purest undecorated form, Pyrex kitchenware has proved to be one of the most enduring classics of the twentieth century.

Tradition triumphant: a chromed electronic wok (*above*) updates an ancient technique, but Chinese steaming baskets (*below*) remain popular.

CURRENT TRENDS AND FUTURE DEVELOPMENTS

Looking back over developments in the modern age, it is striking how excellence in kitchen product manufacturing has expressed national characteristics but has not been restricted to just a couple of nations. From Kenwood in Britain and Braun in Germany to Le Creuset and Sabatier in France, Alessi and Sambonet in Italy, and Tupperware and Pyrex in the USA, innovation in design has been evenly distributed. Today, of course, the influence of the East is strong, which explains why such natural cooking methods as steaming have enjoyed so strong a revival.

Indeed there is currently a deliberate reaction in the kitchen against the synthetic and a return to the natural and organic. The natural warmth of nineteenth-century kitchens has made a comeback, and nineteenth-century cooking methods too in many cases. We have become suspicious of the pre-packaged food industry. This explains the popularity of machines that make real coffee, pasta and ice cream. It also explains why the Japanese should introduce a home bread-maker.

Of course technological sophistication will continue. The microwave will not go away and many age-old vessels will be reinterpreted in a high-tech way: the new electric version of the Chinese wok has a raised cover, for instance, so it can act as a mini-oven. But many traditional gadgets will remain, simply because they cannot be improved upon. Styles and materials may change but who would bet against the old-fashioned potato peeler still being around in the twenty-first century?

Old-fashioned potato peeler: an example of pure function that has endured.

The use of machines and appliances in the modern kitchen has increased dramatically as technology opens up new possibilities. The development of microchip electronics and super-tough engineering plastics have contributed to food-processing inventions with the capacity to shred, chop and slice at a rate unthinkable in the labour-intensive kitchens of the nineteenth century.

Yet alongside technical advances, there has been an enduring interest in the simple, functional machines that are nothing more than an extension of the human hand: the hand-cranked Victorian Spong coffee mill, for example, or the Imperia pasta-making machine of 1929, which essentially replicates the ancient method of hand-stretching strips of dough.

COFFEE MILL
Spong c. 1875

British manufacturer Spong was established in 1856 and became famous for supplying mincing machines to Queen Victoria. Its traditional hand-operated coffee grinder is still popular today, although more for decorative than functional reasons. It is made of stove-enamelled cast iron and steel, with gold lacquer lettering applied by hand, and claims an advantage over modern machines because it grinds the coffee beans into granules rather than smashing them. Spong has been taken over by Salter Housewares, who now make the machine.

MOCCA COFFEE GRINDER
KMV Germany c. 1930

An early use of Bakelite moulding material in kitchen machines, this German product is a lighter, simpler and more sophisticated update on the Spong coffee mill. The two-part housing indicates engineering precision. But the handle on top is in the style of an old spice mill reflecting the centuries-old tradition of coffee-making.

SALUTA No. 584 ELECTRIC TOASTER

made in Britain c. 1930
The primitive structure of this early toaster recalls its origins in the medieval toasting fork. Four rotating wire toast-holders surround a central, cylindrical heating element. The toaster is made of nickel-plated metal with a black circular Bakelite switch on top. This particular toaster was discovered in an auction by Sir Terence Conran and donated to the Design Museum in London.

EMPIRE JUBILEE CREAM-MAKER

Bel 1936
Collectors scour markets for undamaged originals of this classic British-made Bel cream-maker. Comprising a glass container, aluminium handle and urea-formaldehyde top (which was produced in a variety of mottled colours), the Bel machine emulsifies butter and milk to make cream when the lever is vigorously pumped for a few minutes. Its form reflects the refinement in kitchen products which took place in the 1930s.

KALORIK TOASTER
made in Belgium 1940s

More care was taken with the appearance of the toaster as the machine was 'boxed in'. This Belgian model is made of chromed metal with pierced side decoration symbolizing heat and flames. It has insulating Bakelite handles and integral feet, suggesting far greater attention to safety, allowing no opportunity for hands to get trapped in the mechanism. The overall design makes it look much more like a fully functional domestic appliance.

TOASTER
vernacular 1940s

This toaster by an unknown maker is now on show in the London Science Museum and is typical of the 1940s. Its appearance suggests an affinity with the A100 Turn-Over Toaster of 1947, British manufacturer Kenwood's first product, but it is an earlier, cruder model. Like the Kenwood, the bread must be turned over by hand; however there are no slots in which to place it, gates at either side must be opened to insert the slices.

Nevertheless, there is an elegance in the visual composition.

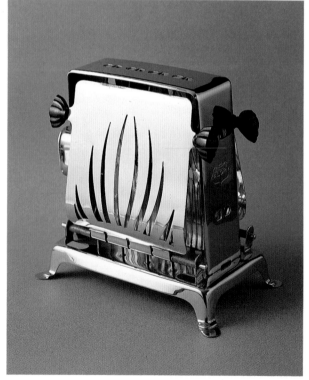

CLEM TOASTER

AB Metal Products 1952

The pioneer American design consultants of the 1930s and 1940s had a passion for streamlining. That, and the rise of auto styling, influenced the look of British domestic products at the time. This toaster reflects the trend. It is also notable for the amount of Bakelite used in its construction: the synthetic proved an excellent insulator as more homes were connected to the mains electricity supply.

TOASTER

Siemens 1959

The evolution of the modern toaster is heralded in this chromed-steel West German model. There are as yet no slots on top to insert bread: side doors are opened by using the Bakelite handles. But the streamlined styling is totally in keeping with the development of the Rationalist form of the modern, technological kitchen. It also represents a more safety-conscious approach with heating elements well hidden.

MULTIPRESS MP3 JUICE EXTRACTOR
Jürgen Greubel for Braun 1957

Part of Braun's 'motorized kitchen collection' and matched in colour and shape to the company's famous Kitchen Machine of the same year, this 1957 electric juice extractor reflects the Modernist design aesthetic for which Braun is renowned. The juice container is made of a plastics material called styrene acrylonitrile; a sturdy rubber base ensures stability; and smooth surfaces enable ease of cleaning. The MP3 is a significant technical update on earlier models with a moveable nozzle, stronger motor and the ability to process more fruit down a broader channel. It demonstrates the formal and uncompromising values of Functionalism which were developed as a matter of corporate policy by Braun designers Fritz Eichler, Dieter Rams and Hans Gugelot in 1955 under the watchful eyes of Artur and Erwin Braun.

MULTIRAPID MXI MIXING SYSTEM

Braun 1950

An early food processor designed in-house by Braun engineers, the MXI could mix, knead, shred and mince food. It is made of steel and dye-cast aluminium with a pressed glass bowl and used centrifuge-operated attachments. The machine became a feature in many German homes.

JUICE-O-MAT LEMON SQUEEZER

made in USA 1950s

Streamlined in chromed metal, this lemon squeezer combined elements of jukebox and robot in its appearance, as kitchen machines rapidly cast off anonymous functionality in favour of personality styling. The Juice-o-Mat has been much imitated, especially in cheap cast aluminium emanating from Taiwan. The real thing, though, is worth having.

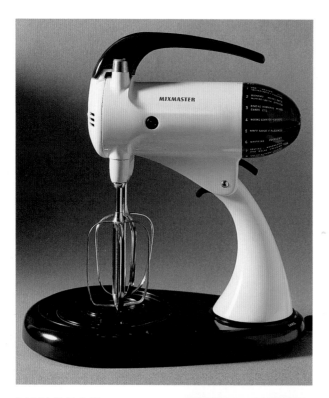

KM321 KITCHEN MACHINE
Gerd Alfred Muller for Braun 1957

The quintessential Braun product – white, plain, smooth, unified and technically perfect – the KM321 Kitchen Machine has clean lines and entirely appropriate balanced proportions. It appears self-contained, almost introverted, in comparison to the extrovert black and white presence of the Sunbeam Mixmaster (*left*), and was unlike any other kitchen machine on the market at the time. The surfaces are easy to clean and all parts can be assembled without screws.

SUNBEAM MIXMASTER
Sunbeam Electric 1955

Manufactured in Glasgow, this elegant electric mixer proved a major seller. Within four years of its launch it held 35 per cent of the market. The Sunbeam mixer combines technical power with visual impact. Its pronounced curves owe much to trends in auto styling of the period, while the black rotating speed control is accessible and pleasing to use.

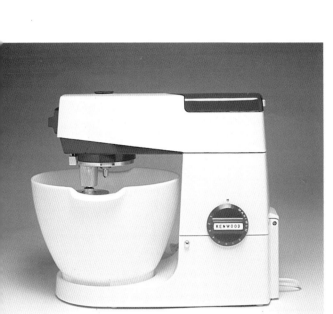

KENWOOD CHEF
Kenneth Grange for Kenwood 1960

The strong influence of Braun is evident in this acclaimed 1960 redesign of the famous Kenwood Chef, first launched in 1950. Kenneth Grange of the Pentagram design group created the archetypal look of an all-purpose machine which became standard in British kitchens. Grange produced the new design in just four days. In that time he was able to build only half a model so he improvised using a mirror.

MAGIMIX FOOD PROCESSOR
Magimix 1978

A new concept in food preparation to revolutionize the kitchen, devised by the French – who else? The Magimix cuisine system offered greater sophistication and finer control in grating, slicing, mixing, chopping and liquidizing materials. The machine's ability to process large amounts accurately was seized on by the world's top chefs, who brought the Magimix into the public eye. Its bowls are made from the same engineering plastics as the windows of Concorde.

ELECTRONIC TOASTER

Braun late 1980s

The most sophisticated toaster of the late 1980s has microchip control to enable variable browning while the plastic housing and wire guards, where the bread is inserted, reflect a safety-conscious attitude. This is the epitomy of the rational, functional Braun approach to white goods – a white box. You cannot fault the correctness of the technical approach, but isn't it just a little boring? The machine certainly lacks the evocative presence and personality of earlier toasters.

TOASTER

Dualit c. 1955

Consumer boredom with white boxes has led to a dramatic revival of interest in this classic British stainless-steel toaster which is unchanged since the 1950s. Aimed initially at the catering trade, its bold hand-finished appearance has made it a high-style object for the home. There are six- four- and two-slot Dualit models. A pull-out crumb tray enables easy cleaning, and a neon indicator glows during toasting.

IMPERIA PASTA-MAKER
Industria Produtti Stampati 1929

Making fresh pasta by hand has recently enjoyed a revival in the home – and with it this classic machine from the 1920s. It was developed in chromium-plated steel by an Italian named Boschis and was originally called the Americanina before being renamed the Imperia in 1937. Various attachments and cutters roll out pasta in flat sheets of six different thicknesses.

MAGIMIX GRANDE FAMILLE 3500
Magimix 1988–9

The late 1980s model from Magimix offers new attachments which enable accurate processing of small amounts of food in the home, in contrast to the company's first systems which were designed for chefs preparing large quantities in restaurants. The touch-sensitive controls indicate how far food processors have come since the 1950s.

Tradition and innovation coexist in the world of kitchen gadgetry. High-density plastics and digital electronics have brought us many attractive new labour-saving devices. Yet traditional cast-iron beam-balance scales remain popular on account of their durability and accuracy, and nobody has bettered the carbon-steel cutting edge of Sabatier knives, which were first developed in the 1880s.

Where the greatest changes have been felt is in the transformation of kitchen utensils from functional products to sculptural objects, aesthetic statements and fashion accessories. Hammarplast's Soft kitchen set, Guzzini's Atelier 75 utensils and Bodum's egg cup clearly indicate the new atmosphere in the kitchen and our revised attitudes to preparing and serving food that have resulted.

SABATIER KITCHEN KNIVES

Maxime Girard 1885

Sabatier kitchen knives have been symbols of technical precision and design excellence for more than a century. Manufactured in Thiers, the knife-making capital of France, Sabatier products were first favoured by leading French chefs and have since become the professional's choice around the world. They are machine-made, in both carbon steel and stainless steel, and hand finished. An integral bolster at the base of the blade gives balance and increases strength. The handles, fashioned in rosewood or Kemetal plastic, are secured with brass rivets which add a decorative touch to a supremely functional product. Today more than a dozen companies have the right to use the Sabatier name, but Maxime Girard maintains the closest links with the original family of knife-makers.

BEAM-BALANCE SCALES

F J Thornton & Co c. 1900

A familiar sight in kitchens at the turn of the century, reproductions of this Victorian design in cast iron and brass remain popular today. The accuracy of beam-balance scales has ensured their endurance despite the development of slimmer electronic scales. British company F J Thornton has specialized in making kitchen scales of this kind for more than 50 years.

KITCHEN UTENSILS

Henry Dreyfuss for Washburn 1936

This range of utilitarian kitchen utensils by one of the USA's most famous pioneering design consultants was developed to be sold piece by piece for only 10 or 15 cents each. The tapering handles were designed in turned wood to increase comfortable use, and each utensil was produced in four separate sizes, each differently proportioned. In all, the range comprised about 50 pieces, from spoons and spatulas to ice picks.

LEMON SQUEEZER
Gino Colombini for Kartell 1958

Designed in Kastilene low-density polyethylene, this is a fine example of how the Italian company Kartell made synthetics highly acceptable for domestic use in the 1950s. The product, which won a Compasso d'Oro industrial-design prize in 1959, is brilliantly functional. The halved lemon is pushed down onto a sharply fretted pivot and covered by a ribbed cap which is turned to press the pulp dry. Channels in the pivot allow the juice to flow into the container below.

O-SERIES SCISSORS
Olaf Backstrom for Fiskars 1963

The Fiskars company has been making scissors in Finland since 1830, but these stainless-steel, general-purpose kitchen scissors broke new ground in their use of ABS plastics for the handles and sound ergnomic principles to achieve improved performance. Designer Olaf Backstrom carved the initial prototypes in wood. Widely regarded as the best household scissors manufactured anywhere in the world, the O-series has been widely imitated. Today they are made by Fiskars for Wilkinson Sword.

COLANDER
KS 1036
Gino Colombini for
Kartell 1960

Another milestone product in Kartell's pioneering programme of plastics objects for domestic use, this carefully moulded colander was first produced in Eltex low-pressure polyethylene. Gino Colombini was Kartell's technical director at the time. The combination of vertical fissures and a network pattern of tiny square holes in the base has a functional rationale – aiding the flow-through of water as well as giving a lighter, more pleasing appearance. Square holes also resulted in a less expensive moulding process.

KITCHEN SCALES
Marco Zanuso for Terraillon c. 1973

Milanese consultant Marco Zanuso dramatically refashioned the kitchen scale with this popular French-made product comprising two ABS mouldings, a magnified clear plastics weight indicator and a pan that also acts as a lid for compact storage. So new was the concept when the scale was launched that many people were initially mystified by its appearance. Terraillon's image of functional modernity, first developed by Zanuso, is still visible in recent products, such as the kitchen timer (*below*).

PROFESSIONAL KNIFE RANGE
Robert Welch for Kitchen Devils 1979

This upmarket range of British knives for the more serious cook combines visual elegance with functional balance. The blades are made of surgical steel which is heat treated and hand whetted to provide lasting hardness. Made of polypropylene with additives, the handles are insert moulded onto tangs then hand finished with brass rivets. The collection won a British Design Council award in 1984 and epitomizes Welch's craftsmanlike approach to industrial-product design.

SCREWPULL
Herbert Allen for Hallen 1979

The Screwpull has become the standard way to extract corks from wine bottles in the USA. Designed by a retired Texan engineer who developed a passion for wine after a career spent drilling in the oil industry, the device has a polycarbonate frame and handle. Its most important feature is the central helical screw with a Teflon coating.

MICROTOUCH SCALE
Design Partners for Tefal 1986

Still the most advanced scale at the end of the 1980s, this product was developed by a French consultancy. It incorporates patented computer-sensitive weighing features, including a facility to convert recipes automatically for any number of people and even speaks to the user: an electric tone indicates when the required amount has been placed on the scale. The scale incorporates a hygienic ABS plastics housing.

SOFT KITCHEN UTENSIL SET
Karl-Axel Andersson and Morgan Ferm for Hammarplast 1987

The Soft collection marks a step forward in aesthetic quality allied to practicality, presenting the kitchen utensil as sculptural object. Designed in nylon by an engineer (Andersson) and a craftsman (Ferm), the range is non-stick and heat resistant: its ability to withstand temperatures of 200°C (400°F) makes it suitable for use in microwaves. Danish Hammarplast has been making plastics for over 40 years.

ELECTRONIC SCALE
Nick Holland Design Group for Waymaster

1988

Entirely designed and manufactured in Britain, this electronic scale marks the growing sophistication of mass-market kitchen products. It incorporates a new, patented weighing system using a form of strain gauge. Waymaster's own electronics engineers developed the technical innovation, while consultant Nick Holland created a product design with a sympathethic curve in an ABS plastics moulding, that portrayed a non-elitist marketing image.

ATELIER 75
Bruno Gecchelin for Guzzini 1989

This range of four utensils was designed to commemorate the seventy-fifth anniversary of the founding of the famous Italian manufacturing company Guzzini. The sculpted ABS plastics handles pay homage to four inspirational artists: Moore, Picasso, Miro and Boccioni and the result is a unique collection reflecting the creative spirit of the Guzzini brothers.

DIGITAL TIMER
E K Bengt for EKS 1989

Moulded in ABS plastics, this Swiss-made digital timer could signal the elevation of the kitchen gadget to fashion accessory. It comes with clips and magnets and can be fastened to your clothing as you move around the house or attached to the refrigerator. Either way, style and wit have been injected into a usually mundane object.

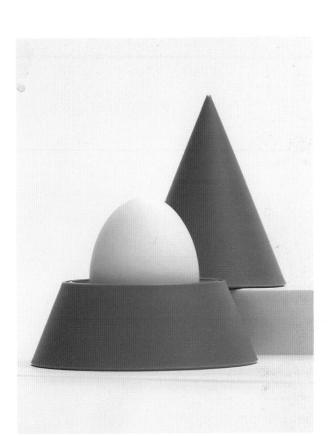

EGG CUP
**Maya Kissoczy for
Bodum** 1985

Sometimes the simplest ideas are the best. This ingenious polypropylene egg cup has a salt cellar as an integral part of its conical cover and holds variously sized eggs. It is a pleasing decorative object even when not in use. Its elevation to cult status hás confirmed the ability of Swiss company Bodum to convey style through simplicity.

Where professional chefs lead, committed home cooks will follow. Many of the most popular mass-market cookware ranges of this century owe their success to initial patronage by the great and the good in the kitchen. Passing design fads are less likely to be observed in conducting the serious business of preparing food but genuine technological innovation is swiftly appreciated and adopted.

And there has been no shortage of breakthroughs, especially in materials technology, where heat-resistant glass, stainless steel, nylon and acetal hard-anodized aluminium have all made their mark. The particular way in which designers have exploited these advances has determined the classic quality of modern cookware, each range with its individual characteristics and appeal.

COOKWARE
Le Creuset 1925

The famous heavy different-coloured pans of Le Creuset are made of vitreous enamelled cast-iron, a material used for cookware since the Middle Ages. But what has characterized Le Creuset since the company began manufacturing in 1925 at its Fresnoy-Le Grand foundry at St Quentin in northern France has been the degree of hand-finishing which ensures that each pan attains the highest technical standards. Le Creuset products are intended to last a lifetime. Top-sellers for more than 60 years, the pans are coated with thick enamel.

TUPPERWARE
Earl Tupper for Tupperware Co. 1968

These dessert (*front*) and parfait (*rear*) sets with airtight lids and frosted finish are from the polyethylene range launched in 1946. The hygienic, lightweight, unbreakable containers were developed in the USA by chemist and engineer Earl Tupper, whose pioneering work created a potent symbol of consumer culture and achieved global success after World War Two.

KUBUS CONTAINERS
Wilhelm Wagenfeld for the Lausitzer Glassworks 1938
Modernist design theory was applied to kitchen pots by Bauhaus student Wilhelm Wagenfeld. This set of modular storage containers in pressed glass fits together to form a perfect cube. Included in the collection are pouring vessels such as a teapot and milk jug, with integral moulded lips and handles. Kubus is now a rare collector's item.

MARGRETHE MIXING BOWLS

Bjorn and Sigvard Bernadotte for Rosti

1950

An early example of the use of melamine in kitchen bowls, this design for Danish manufacturer Rosti has rarely been bettered. The designers paid close attention to ergonomics in creating a modular range of sizes ideal for kitchen use. Each bowl is moulded in Mepal melamine with a lip to ensure a firm grip in use and a rubber non-slip ring on the base.

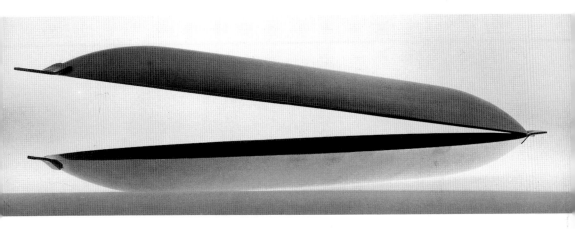

FISH DISH
Roberto Sambonet for Sambonet 1954

This innovative fish dish by Roberto Sambonet demonstrated previously unappreciated aesthetic values in stainless steel and became a potent symbol of its sculptural potential. Shaped by a special process involving the use of compressed air, the design's pure, streamlined form won a Compasso d'Oro industrial-design award.

PYREX DISH
Milner Gray and Kenneth Lamble for James Jobling & Co 1955

Pyrex was developed in the USA at the Corning Glassworks in 1915 and became the trade name for a renowned range of borosilicate glass heat-resistant oven-to-table vessels. Sunderland manufacturer Jobling was awarded a licence to make Pyrex dishes in Britain in 1921. This pressed-glass dish with a broad handle was designed by Gray and Lamble of Design Research Unit.

LE PENTOLE
Niki Sala for Industrie Casalinghi Mori 1979

An important addition to the modern cooking scene, Le Pentole was developed in Italy to enable steam-cooking in keeping with healthier eating trends. A stacking system made of extremely tough, non-scratch stainless steel, the range has innumerable advantages. No heat or energy is wasted because the pans can be stacked up to five tiers high. Different cooking techniques can be employed simultaneously in different tiers and one dish can be kept warm while another cooks below it. Lids can be rested on the handles while stirring. The permutations are truly remarkable and Le Pentole has achieved international acclaim among serious cooks.

ELYSEE LINE
Cuisinox 1981

Cuisinox was established by Frenchman Jean Couzon, a maker of handcrafted cutlery since the 1930s, to achieve standards in stanless-steel cookware normally associated with silverware. A high-tech factory was built near Vichy in 1975 and the Elysée line was designed to appeal to both chefs and home cooks. The 40-piece range shows great attention to detail: pans have a highly polished hand finish and excellent pouring lips.

WORKING KITCHEN RANGE
Conran Design Group for Crayonne 1981

Made in polypropylene and nylon, this coordinated kitchen preparation system was developed by Conran for British retailers Boots and Timothy Whites. Its style set the tone for plastics kitchenware in the 1980s.

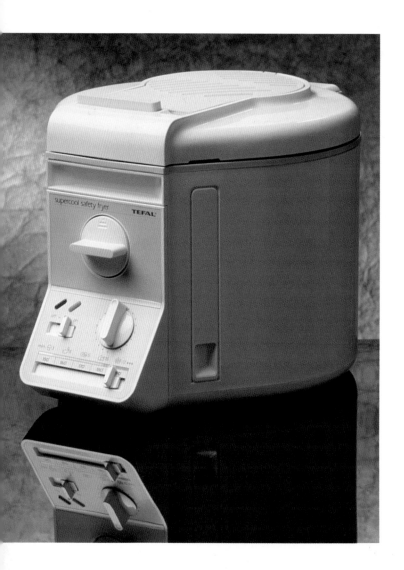

SUPERCOOL DEEPFAT FRYER
Seymour Powell for Tefal 1988

This imposing machine was developed in response to a new trend in 1980s cooking – the preparation of deep-fried foods using an electric frier. It is moulded in polypropylene and has an aluminium inner liner which holds the boiling oil. Utilizing cool-to-touch plastics and fail-safe systems to ensure complete safety, the frier can be touched without harm even when frying at 190°C (375°F). It is one of many kitchen appliances designed for French company Tefal by British product consultants Richard Seymour and Dick Powell, whose emphatic, high-tech styling has made its mark internationally.

SIEVE AND COLANDER
Richard Sapper for Alessi 1986
Both pieces are from the Alessi Chef's range, designed in stainless steel by Richard Sapper with consultant Gualtiero Marchesi. The range extends the manufacturer's exploration of beautiful new forms in kitchen products under its Officina Alessi trademark, best known for the 1983 Tea & Coffee Piazza series of silver services by 11 international architects.

CALPHALON
Commercial Aluminium Cookware 1978
This American range developed in Ohio in the late 1970s is made of hard-anodized aluminium. Hard-anodizing is an electro-chemical process which transforms the surface of aluminium to a glass-like, non-porous finish which is harder than steel. Calphalon pans, aimed at serious cooks, have a tough non-stick finish and are impossible to scratch.

The culture and technology of coffee-making was the focus for much product innovation in the eighteenth and nineteenth centuries. But it has been in recent times that the equipment at the heart of this special social ritual has been truly reinvented with the advances in electrics, heat-resistant glass, plastics, aluminium and stainless steel.

If names like Gaggia and Pavoni evoke the European coffee-bar beat scene of the 1950s and 1960s, then we must look earlier to the pioneering efforts of Behrens, Calimani and Bialetti for the forerunners to the products which now adorn our kitchens. Kettles, coffeepots and flasks have today become fashionable, sculptural objects which regularly cross the threshold into tableware. Yet they must continue to operate within strict functional parameters and so they are still a focus of a designer's ingenuity.

ELECTRIC KETTLE
Peter Behrens
for AEG 1908

A milestone consumer product by the founding father of modern industrial design, this nickel-plated steel kettle was designed just a year after Peter Behrens was appointed artistic adviser to the giant AEG company in Berlin. Distinguished by a circular base, octagonal sectioned body and wicker-covered loop handle, the kettle's functional approach demonstrates the way Behrens modified the Art Nouveau style to create a more geometric, Modernist design for everyday objects.

SIPHON-ACTION PERCOLATOR
British c. 1890

This percolator operates on the principle of vacuum siphon coffee-making invented in the 1850s. Boiling water is poured over ground coffee in the left-hand glass flask, while steam generated by hot water in the right-hand china flask creates a vacuum. The liquid coffee is drawn up through the siphon into the china flask.

VACUUM FLASK

Thermos 1930

The British Thermos company developed such a reputation for producing quality vacuum flasks that the name has now become generic, like Hoover for vacuum cleaners. This elegant, streamlined design with stylized handles was made of urea formaldehyde – the most sophisticated plastics material of the period with heat-retaining properties – with a cork and urea-formaldehyde stopper. Its striking presence is some indication of why Thermos products became so popular and successful, and why they now fetch high prices among collectors. First established in 1925, the company was formally registered as Thermos (1925) Ltd.

LA CAFETIERE
Calimani 1933

The first Cafetière plunge-pot coffee-maker was developed by an Italian named Calimani in 1933. The principle – whereby a filter is manually plunged down through infused coffee – came into use in cafés after 1945 and achieved its breakthrough in France during the 1950s. Today there are many different types of cafetière on the market, but we can get a clear idea of Calimani's original design from a faithful reproduction by Swiss manufacturer Bodum. The classic French Chambord coffee-maker (shown here) is an elegant piece made of nickel-plated brass and thick borosilicate glass with black Bakelite handles.

MOKA EXPRESS
Alfonso Bialetti for Bialetti 1930s

Bialetti's famous Moka pressure pot marked a change in coffeepot design. It departed radically from the artisan look of earlier designs, featuring an industrial solidity in its heavy cast-aluminium form. As an unusual endorsement of the product a caricature of Bialetti, complete with whiskers, adorned all Moka Express coffeepots and appeared in Television commercials, announcing; 'Making good coffee seems easy, but water and coffee aren't enough. Moka is needed.'

GILDA ESPRESSO MACHINE
Achille Gaggia for Brevetti Gaggia 1952–4

The world's first domestic electric espresso coffee-maker was named after Rita Hayworth's role in the film *Gilda*. With a circular base and levers with Bakelite grips, it looks as though it is about to take flight. Gaggia, a former barman, pioneered the piston-driven espresso machine without steam in the 1940s, and is associated with the rise of coffee-bar culture throughout Europe during the 1950s. His machines evoke the innocence of a lost age.

NEAPOLITAN DRIP POT
Vernacular Naples 1940s
This classic Neapolitan coffeepot derives its design from drip-pots dating back to the eighteenth century. Made of tin or aluminium, it works on the flip-pot principle: when the water boils, the pot is turned upside down and the water filters slowly without pressure through ground coffee held in a central compartment. The process demands skill and dexterity to perform, giving the act a ritualistic character. In 1979 the design was the subject of a well-documented update by Riccardo Dalisi for Alessi.

VACUUM JUG
The British Vacuum Flask Company 1940s
A striking departure in the design of urea-formaldehyde vacuum flasks with its decorative relief pattern and ornate handle, this British vacuum jug was developed to be a social accessory as well as a functional object, proving that attitudes to plastics were changing. It was advertised for use at table, in the nursery and for serving cocktails.

EUROPICCOLA ESPRESSO MACHINE
La Pavoni 1962

The name La Pavoni evoked the spirit of European coffee bars at a time when the hissing steam of espresso machines was a fitting accompaniment to rock'n'roll. This domestic machine in chromed steel with Bakelite screwtops is typical of the era. Its mechanical lever forces hot water through tightly packed coffee. Steam is also created and expelled through a tube, giving the milk its frothy white head.

CONA COFFEE NEW TABLE MODEL
Abram Games for Cona
1959

Designed in 1957 by one of Britain's best-known poster artists and launched two years later, this coffee-maker reflects the streamlined design thinking of the late 1950s. Heat-resistant glass flasks are supported on a cantilevered stand, enabling the coffee-making process to remain in full view. Cona still sells thousands of coffee-makers worldwide.

WHISTLING KETTLE
New-Maid late 1950s
A classic British kitchen kettle with two-tone whistle, it was built to last a lifetime and is now much imitated, particularly by Japanese companies. Its heavy base ensures stability and its Bakelite handle is designed to keep the hand well away from the steam which emerges from its Bakelite spout. New-Maid created a series of attractive colours using a metallized-finish on the quality steel body.

ARABIA COFFEEPOTS
Antti Nurmesniemi for Arabia 1958
Brightly-coloured and made of enamelled-steel, Nurmesniemi's coffeepot became a standard item in many Scandinavian homes and a celebrated example of simple, accessible, modern Finnish design. The water percolates up through ground coffee held in an internal container.

FUTURA FORGETTLE KETTLE
Julius Thalmann for Russell Hobbs 1974–5

This British model, with its smooth, futuristic contours and stainless-steel top, marked a major breakthrough as it was the first automatic kettle with a body moulded in acetal. Now all jug kettles are made of this synthetic, which does not build up limescale in contact with water. Thalmann was an in-house designer at Russell Hobbs.

K3 SERIES KETTLE
Russell Hobbs 1982

Designed in-house, this kitchen workhorse has come to epitomize many of the best, unobtrusive qualities of British design. Made of polished stainless steel with phenolic plastic switch housing and handle, it has a durability and safety which have ensured its continued popularity in the face of more consciously fashionable plastics jug kettles.

CAFETIERE
Richard Sapper for Alessi 1979

This espresso coffee-maker in stainless steel is a piece of sophisticated engineering which is highly complex to produce. Over a hundred operations are required just to finish one pot. Its Milan-based designer, Richard Sapper, was more interested in durability and safety than style. He said of the project: 'I wanted to make something that did not look like a coffeepot because, apart from the Moka, all the others do. This is a little steam engine!' Indeed his uncompromisingly functional cafetière could be regarded as the only natural successor to Bialetti's Moka Express Classic.

KETTLE
Richard Sapper for Alessi 1983

One of the most famous cult objects of the 1980s, this kettle demonstrates Sapper's exploration of the underlying symbolic values of objects and departure from functional values. The stainless-steel kettle has the drawback of heating the lever which releases the spout's lid for pouring. The 'wavy' polyamide-covered handle is surprising, given Sapper's decision to avoid a plastics handle on the Alessi Cafetière four years earlier (because 'sooner or later they all burn'). But its appearance is enchanting, and its brass whistle emits a melodic tone.

KETTLE
Michael Graves for Alessi 1985

Designed in stainless steel with a nylon handle by the USA's leading exponent of Post-Modernist architecture, Graves's high-selling Alessi model swiftly became known as the Bird Kettle on account of its small bird-shaped whistle. The design attracted much criticism from Modernists. But is it really a kitsch object, or a serious design metaphor?

CAFETIERE
Aldo Rossi for Alessi
1988

Calimani's original plunge-pot is given a geometrical late-1980s treatment by Aldo Rossi. The press-filter coffee maker is made of stainless steel and heat-resistant glass. There is a satisfying simplicity in its composition, reflecting Rossi's background as one of Italy's best-known professors of architecture. Rossi began collaborating with the Alessi company on the design of coffee-makers and wrist watches in the 1980s, bringing a characteristic fluency of vision and attention to detail to product development.

ESPRESSO MINI MACHINE
Florian Seiffert for Krups 1985

Technology brought sophisticated miniaturization to the espresso maker. This Krups model is equipped with a powerful steam-pressure system to make four cups at once. There is also a steam pipe to froth up the milk for cappuccinos, but its sleek black image is a far cry from the chrome-plate of the 1940s.

CAFE GOURMET
Lou Beeren for Philips
1988

This top-of-the-range filter coffee-maker reflects the transition of such equipment from kitchen to table as an important social accessory. Made of heat-resistant glass, ABS plastics and chrome-plated steel, it is attractive to the eye and easy to clean. It also incorporates a series of useful technical features, including a swing filter and hot plate. The piece indicates the priority that Philips's industrial-design unit gives to product design.

VACUUM JUG MODERN CLASSICS No 1
Ole Palsby for Alfi Zitzmann 1985

Made of stainless steel with a vacuum glass inner-lining so that no heat is conducted to the handle, this globe-like vacuum jug is based on a simple, economical idea. As Danish industrial designer Ole Palsby, explains 'The sphere is the geometric solid that has the smallest surface and the biggest content'. The jug is made in Germany and is part of the Modern Classics range, which includes pieces in coloured steel and patterned plastics.

VACUUM JUGS
Franz Wulf for Emsa 1988
Studies in pure form and colour, these German vacuum jugs made of ABS plastics represent the ultimate in modern lifestyle accessorizing in the kitchen. This is very much a case of form following fashion. Designer Franz Wulf is head of this private family business which has become a brand leader in Germany. The jugs are packaged and marketed as giftware. They have an eccentricity which reflects Wulf's individualism.

PAPILLON VACUUM JUGS
Furio Minuti for Guzzini
1986 and 1989

A touch of humour is brought to objects which are usually stark, serious and geometric. These jugs, which are part of the Papillon tableware range, have a zoomorphic, whimsical quality. The taller of the two was introduced first; the squatter version came three years later. Guzzini has a long track record in producing quality plastics products.

Formed by Enrico Guzzini in 1911, the company began by working with horn – a forerunner to plastics.

OLAF BACKSTROM

Finnish designer Olaf Backstrom, the man responsible for the classic Fiskars **O-series general-purpose scissors**, was born in 1922. He trained in electrical engineering and spent the first 11 years of his career working as an engineer.

He became increasingly dissatisfied with his work, however, and in 1954 began to design handmade wooden utility objects as a hobby. Four years later he switched entirely from engineering to the more creative dimension of product design when he became an industrial designer at Fiskars.

Backstrom's work for Fiskars was in plastics, although he carved the initial prototypes of the scissors in wood. The milestone scissors project was started in 1961 and completed in 1967. It was preceded by another important design assignment for Fiskars – a melamine tableware collection.

PETER BEHRENS

One of the great industrial-design pioneers of the early twentieth century, Peter Behrens (1868–1940) played a leading role in establishing a Functionalist design ethic in the manufacture of products for the home.

Behrens trained at the art school in Karlsruhe and privately in Düsseldorf and Munich. He joined the avant-garde Munich Secession in 1893 and later contributed to the founding of the Deutscher Werkbund, a German association aimed at uniting art and industry in a focus on the function of products.

In 1907, the same year as the Deutscher Werkbund was established, Behrens became one of the first architect-designers to be employed by a large industrial company when he went to Berlin to take up the post of artistic adviser to the giant industrial combine AEG (Allgemeine Elektrizitäts-Gesellschaft).

He assumed responsibility for AEG's products, buildings and publicity, giving the company its famous corporate identity and overseeing an enormous volume of design work from electric kettles and lamps to catalogues, letterheads and exhibitions.

Walter Gropius, Mies van der Rohe and, very briefly, Le Corbusier all worked as design assistants in the office of Peter Behrens, whose portfolio of achievements at AEG became the standard by which much subsequent twentieth-century design would be judged.

Later in his career, in 1932, Behrens became director of architecture at the Vienna Academy. From 1936 until his death in 1940 he was director of the department of architecture at the Prussian Academy in Berlin.

GINO COLOMBINI

Italian designer Gino Colombini was born in Milan in 1915 and studied for a diploma in master building. From 1933–52 he worked for the architect Franco Albini, designing furniture, as well as public buildings and private houses.

However, Colombini is best known for his work as technical director of the Italian plastics manufacturer Kartell between 1952 and 1961. He was responsible for taking newly-developed plastics materials and creating a technical and aesthetic quality appropriate for use in the home.

A kitchen bucket designed by Colombini won a

Compasso d'Oro award for industrial design in 1955 and further Colombini designs for Kartell won this coveted Italian prize in 1957, 1959 and 1960.

Colombini revealed great precision and subtlety in developing a wide range of Kartell kitchen products in plastics, from soup tureens and colanders to lemon squeezers. He continued his innovative use of plastics as head of the technical office of Polifiber-Renos from 1961 to 1983. Since then he has designed furniture for Vittorio Bonacina.

HENRY DREYFUSS

American industrial-designer Henry Dreyfuss (1904–72) was born into a family which specialized in prop and

costume hire, and he went into the theatre at the age of 17 as a stage designer.

He was destined, however, to become one of the select band of American design consultants who laid the foundations of the modern international design-consultancy business in the 1930s. Together with Raymond Loewy, Walter Dorwin Teague and Norman Bel Geddes (a designer with whom he had worked on several stage shows), Dreyfuss redefined the role of industrial design in American industry during the Depression of the 1930s.

He opened his own design office in 1929, the year of the Wall Street Crash, and his first industrial design exercise was to rework the traditional kitchen storage-jar. He went on to become one of the USA's most powerful and influential designers, creating kitchen utensils for the Washburn Company, vacuum cleaners for Hoover, televisions for RCA, tractors for John Deere and plane interiors for Lockheed.

Dreyfuss's classic 1933 ' telephone handset for Bell endured for decades while his streamlined Hudson locomotive came to be

regarded as the symbol of the USA's New Deal in the 1930s.

Dreyfuss's legacy is a New York practice bearing his name which continues his principles and is highly respected on the American design scene.

ACHILLE GAGGIA

The Italian master of the espresso machine, Achille Gaggia (1895–1961) worked originally as a barman in his native Milan.

Dissatisfied with the burnt and meagre taste of coffee prepared in steam-driven machines, he set about experimenting in his attic with a new method using a piston so that water could be forced through a bed of coffee at high pressure. The result was a fresher cup of coffee with a creamy head.

Gaggia's first experiments with pistons received successful trials in various Milanese coffee bars in 1937–8. But his efforts to develop the first espresso without steam were interrupted by World War Two. However, in 1944, he patented his idea and three years later he set up his own manufacturing company, Brevetti Gaggia, to exploit it.

Gaggia's first machine was called Classico and it could run on gas or electricity. Orders immediately flooded in and successive Gaggia espresso models achieved worldwide sales. In the early 1950s Achille Gaggia named his first domestic electric espresso-maker **Gilda** after the film of the same name starring Rita Hayworth.

In 1962, a year after his death, Brevetti Gaggia moved to new factory premises.

ABRAM GAMES

Veteran British graphic artist Abram Games (b. 1914) is best known for his posters of the 1940s and 1950s for Shell, BP, Guinness, London Transport and the War Office. He became the last master of drawn lithography before the age of photographic communication and his propaganda efforts in the Ministry of Information during World War Two secured his reputation.

Games also explored industrial design, developing a new-look Cona coffee percolator in 1951 and in the early 1960s redesigning the entire mechanism and components of the Gestetner duplicating machine. This

design, however, was not implemented due to Gestetner's death.

He will be best remembered, though, for his war-time posters and for the graphics he devised for the 1951 Festival of Britain, an event of major significance in British post-war design.

BRUNO GECCHELIN

Italian architect and designer Bruno Gecchelin (b. 1939) studied architecture at Milan Polytechnic.

He began his versatile career in 1962 and has worked as a consultant designer for many leading Italian industrial companies. Among his design credits are kitchen utensils for Guzzini, refrigerators and gas cookers for Indesit, furniture for Busnelli and Frau, and lighting for O Luce, Venini and Skipper.

Gecchelin collaborated with Ettore Sottsass on projects for Fiat (the Doima camper and Fiat Panda) and Olivetti (typewriters, calculators and terminals). In 1970 the Olivetti MC27 calculator on which Gecchelin worked was awarded the Compasso d'Oro prize for industrial design.

KENNETH GRANGE

Britain's most important and influential modern industrial-design consultant, Kenneth Grange (b. 1929) is a partner in the Pentagram international design practice, which has offices in London, New York and San Francisco.

Grange was educated at Sir John Cass Foundation School and at Willesden School of Arts and Crafts. For two years from 1947 he trained as a technical illustrator while doing national service in the Royal Engineers. He subsequently worked as an assistant in a number of design and architectural offices before setting up his own consultancy in 1958.

Grange immediately became identified with successful products, redesigning the **Kenwood Chef** in 1960 and creating the Kodak 44A camera in the same year. He went on to design the Venner parking meter, the Parker 25 pen, the British Rail 125 train and Wilkinson Sword razors.

He has played a full part in the institutions of British design, becoming a Royal Designer for Industry in 1969 and the Design Council's industrial design adviser a

decade later. Grange was awarded the CBE in the 1984 New Year's Honours List and served as president of the Chartered Society of Designers in 1987–8.

The irony is that Grange's international career has soared while British industry, where he first earned his reputation, has been largely decimated in recent years. Grange now works extensively for Japanese customers.

MICHAEL GRAVES

American architect Michael Graves (b. 1934) has exerted a major influence on international design as a leading spokesman for Post-Modernism.

His Portland Public Services Building in Oregon, completed in 1982, epitomizes his approach to decoration and symbolism in buildings. But Graves has also explored a Post-Modern world in kitchenware, tableware, furniture and interiors with his work for Alessi, Memphis and Sunar.

A gifted artist whose architectural drawings are collectors' items and sell as such, Graves is professor of architecture at Princeton University, where he has taught since 1962.

Graves trained at Harvard, rising to prominence in the 1970s. Although his forays into 'kitsch' kettles and coffee sets have been heavily criticized by the architectural establishment, his contribution to building design in the Post-Modern 1980s was considerable.

MILNER GRAY

One of the grand old men of modern British design, Milner Gray (b. 1899) played a leading role in the development of the design-consultancy industry in the United Kingdom.

He helped found the world's first professional organization for designers, the Society of Industrial Artists, in 1930 (later known as the Society of Industrial Artists and Designers, it has since been granted a royal charter). During World War Two he and partner Misha Black designed propaganda exhibitions for the Ministry of Information, and they went on to set up Britain's first modern design consultancy, Design Research Unit (DRU) in 1943.

Gray and Black were much influenced by the example of Loewy, Dreyfuss and other American consultants during the 1930s and set about making DRU the best-known design consultancy of the era.

Milner Gray is best known as a graphic designer – the British Rail corporate identity is an outstanding example of DRU's work. But he also worked in kitchenware, developing prototype kitchens for the 1946 Britain Can Make It exhibition and Pyrex ovenware for Corning.

NICK HOLLAND

British industrial designer Nick Holland (b. 1946) earned a distinction at the Royal College of Art before embarking on a career in industry and consultancy.

He worked initially in the hydraulic equipment sector

before becoming general manager of Design Objectives, a small company marketing home accessories, in 1973. Homewares subsequently became the focus of his work.

From 1976 to 1982 Holland was in charge of design development for Staffordshire Potteries, a manufacturer of modern ceramic tableware. He established his own design manufacturing company, Nicholas John, in 1982. The following year he set up a consultancy, Nick Holland Design Group, in Cardiff.

Holland's design firm is now active in a wide range of fields, including kitchenware. Nick Holland himself combines consultancy with extensive lecturing commitments and is regarded as one of the most dynamic figures in contemporary British design.

ANTTI NURMESNIEMI

One of the leading names of Finnish design, Antti Nurmesniemi (b. 1927) studied interior design at art college in Helsinki. Upon graduation in 1951 he worked in the architectural office of Viljo Rewell, where he designed a wide range of interiors for banks, restaurants and hotels.

In 1954 Nurmesniemi went to Milan to work for architect Giovanni Romano for two years. All of this experience proved invaluable in setting up his own studio on his return to Finland in 1956.

Nurmesniemi specialized in product design and interiors, and went on to design best-selling coffeepots, cooking utensils and chairs which combined traditional Finnish grace with Modernist authority.

Nurmesniemi has been one of the driving forces of Finnish design for more than 30 years, a prolific international prize-winner and a tireless lecturer. His furniture collaborations with his wife Vuokko Eskolin-Nurmesniemi, who has her own company called Vuokko, in particular reveal the essential character of a designer whose name is associated with the best of Finnish Modernism.

DIETER RAMS

The most important industrial designer of post-war Germany, Dieter Rams (b. 1932) has been responsible for the pure Functionalist aesthetic of Braun domestic products.

Rams's first contact with design was in his grandfather's carpentry business. He was apprenticed as a joiner and later studied architecture and design at Wiesbaden School of Art, in the town where he was born.

He worked initially for the architectural firm of Otto Apel and collaborated with the American designers Skidmore, Owings and Merrill, who were involved in US consulate buildings in West Germany at the time.

Then, in 1955, he was appointed chief designer at Braun AG. Rams developed an austere, restrained house style which combined clarity and simplicity with sculptural presence. By 1959 a large number of Braun products were on display in the New York Museum of Modern Art.

Nobody exemplifies the effect of the Modern Movement on manufacturing industry more than Dieter Rams. In his work can be seen the development of German Functionalism from the founding of the Deutscher Werkbund in 1907 and the Bauhaus in 1919. Rams himself joined the Deutscher Werkbund in the 1950s.

Today he undertakes a gruelling lecturing and consultancy schedule. Braun is now owned by the American company Gillette and Rams is extending his principles to industry in the USA.

ALDO ROSSI

Leading Italian architect Aldo Rossi was born in Milan in 1931. He began his prodigious career in 1956 working with Ignazio Gradella and later collaborated with Marco Zanuso.

Rossi has combined architecture with product design, education and journalism. He was editor-in-chief of *Casabella-Continuita* until 1964, after which he designed many buildings. From 1975 he held the chair of architectural composition at Venice University, one of several academic distinctions he has gained.

During the 1980s Rossi collaborated with Alessi, designing coffee sets and wrist watches for the manufacturer.

ROBERTO SAMBONET

Italian commercial artist, painter and product designer Roberto Sambonet was born in Vercelli in 1924 into the famous Sambonet family of tableware and kitchenware manufacturers.

The Sambonet family were originally goldsmiths and silversmiths who arrived in Vercelli, between Milan and Turin, from France in the mid-nineteenth century. The first Sambonet hallmark was stamped on a piece of silverware in 1859.

Roberto Sambonet joined the family firm in 1953, at a time when the company was first exploring the use of stainless steel. He had trained under the great Alvar Aalto in Finland and worked at the Sao Paolo Museum of Modern Art in Brazil.

His approach to household objects was to strip them of all unnecessary decoration to create pure, streamlined, dignified forms. A **fish-serving dish** he designed in 1954 became a symbol of the new

elegance in stainless steel and won a Compasso d'Oro award.

In 1970 the entire Sambonet range won a Compasso d'Oro award, proof of the way his creative design ideas had influenced production.

RICHARD SAPPER

Richard Sapper (b. 1932) studied mechanical engineering and worked for Mercedes-Benz in Stuttgart before leaving his native West Germany to settle in Milan in 1958.

Sapper worked in the office of Gio Ponti and collaborated with Marco Zanuso on a series of objects which have become high-design cult favourites among collectors. A whistling **kettle** for Alessi, a 'black' television set for Brion Vega and the famous Tizio desk light for Artemide are among Sapper's best-known pieces.

He brought to Milan the engineering precision of Germany and married it with the more symbolic and sensual values evident in the best Italian design. Two contradictory strands now dominate his work. One is a studied seriousness – Sapper

has been a consultant to IBM since 1981. The other is a wilful playfulness, in which Formalism takes precedence over function.

RICHARD SEYMOUR AND DICK POWELL

British designers Richard Seymour (b. 1953) and Dick Powell (b. 1951) formed the Seymour Powell product design consultancy in London in 1983.

Seymour studied graphic design at the Central School of Art and Design and at the Royal College of Art before working as a creative director in advertising and as a freelance art director on various advertising and new product development projects.

Powell trained as an industrial designer at Manchester Polytechnic and

the Royal College of Art before combining design consultancy with part-time teaching and writing.

Their partnership has proved to be one of the most effective in contemporary British industrial design: each brings a different viewpoint to the discipline. Seymour Powell, which employs 18 designers, now works for a number of leading international companies, including the French domestic-wares company Tefal and Japanese motorcycle manufacturer Yamaha.

EARL TUPPER

The celebrated American inventor of Tupperware, Earl Tupper (1907–83) grew up on a farm in Massachusetts.

He was working as a chemist and engineer, during the infancy of plastics in the early 1940s, when he chanced upon a way to inject polyethylene into moulds and so to create kitchen containers with an airtight seal which were lightweight, flexible and unbreakable.

Tupper formed the Tupper Plastics Company in 1942 and opened his first factory in South Grafton, a small town in Massachusetts. It was the

start of a multi-million-dollar empire. He also exploited subsequent innovations in plastics, marketing his products via a series of 'Tupperware parties' in people's homes across the States. This concept spread around the world.

Tupper himself has been described variously as an eccentric, a hermit, an oddball and a perfectionist. In 1955 he personally masterminded a move to a larger factory but three years later he abruptly sold his business to the Rexall Drug Corp. and disassociated himself from the product which still bears his name.

In retirement Tupper confessed he was disenchanted with his country, claiming that 'America has lost its objective: to do things with verve'. He died of a heart attack in Costa Rica.

WILHELM WAGENFELD

One of the most famous of the Bauhaus students, German designer Wilhelm Wagenfeld (b. 1900) has assumed an importance in twentieth-century design which rivals that of his tutor Laszlo Moholy-Nagy.

Throughout a long career in design education and practice, Wagenfeld's utilitarian objects for the home have been popular and accessible without sacrificing his uncompromising belief in the social and aesthetic ideals of the Modern movement.

Unlike many of his Bauhaus mentors, Wagenfeld remained in Germany throughout the rise and fall of Nazism. He taught at Berlin's Staatliche Kunsthochschule (State College of Art) from 1931 to 1935 and then spent time at the Lausitz Glassworks.

He later became professor of the Hochschule fur Bildende Kunste in Berlin, and in 1954 he set up his own studio in Stuttgart. Wagenfeld has worked for such leading manufacturers as Rosenthal and Braun. His kitchen storage jars and tea-sets in heat-resistant glass have become landmarks of twentieth-century homewares design.

ROBERT WELCH

Leading British industrial designer and silversmith Robert Welch was born in Hereford in 1929.

He studied painting at Malvern School of Art and silversmithing at Birmingham College of Art before undertaking further training at the Royal College of Art (RCA), where he specialized in stainless-steel design.

When he left the RCA in 1955, Welch was appointed design consultant to Old Hall Tableware, a position he held for 28 years until the company ceased trading. Among his many designs for Old Hall was a stainless-steel toast rack, which won a British Design Award in 1958, and the Alveston cutlery range which won the same award in 1965.

Upon graduation, Welch also set up his own workshop at Chipping Camden in Gloucestershire, adding a retail showroom to sell his work in 1969.

He has consistently divided his career between product design for manufacturers all over the world and commissioned and personal silverwork. His consumer products have included kitchen knives and cast-iron cookware, ceramic tableware and cutlery, alarm clocks and lighting. In 1965 Welch was elected a Royal Designer for Industry and he went on to produce more classic lines, including the **Professional** **Kitchen Devils range** of 1979. Many of his designs have become collectors' items and are now on display in leading museums.

MARCO ZANUSO

Italian architect and designer Marco Zanuso is an important propagandist for Italian design. He graduated in architecture from Milan Polytechnic before joining its teaching staff.

In the years of reconstruction after 1945 he played an important part in establishing Milan as the world's design capital – editing magazines (including *Domus* and *Casabella*), organizing theoretical debates and designing successive Milan Triennales.

As a consultant Zanuso has designed factories and offices for Olivetti in Brazil and furniture for Arflex and Kartell. His celebrated partnership with the German Richard Sapper has resulted in a number of design classics, including the 'black' television set for Brion Vega.

Page numbers in *italic* refer to the illustrations

AB Metal Products, 27
AEG, 9, 58
Alessi, 21, 55, 66–8
Allen, Herbert, 41
Andersson, Karl-Axel, 42
appliances, 23–33
Arabia, 64

Backstrom, Olaf, 38, 72
Bauhaus, 9, 10
Beeren, Lou, 69
Behrens, Peter, 9–10, 57, 58, 72
Bel, 25
Bengt, E K, 44
Bernadotte, Bjorn and Sigvard, 50
Bialetti, Alfonso, 57, 61
Bodum, 35, 45
Braun, 8, 8, 12–13, 21, 28–9, 30, 32
British Vacuum Flask Company, 62

Calimani, 57, 60
Calphalon, 55
coffeepots and kettles, 16, 57–71
Colombini, Gino, 12, 38–9, 72–3
Cona, 63
Conran, Terence, 13–14, 13
Conran Design Group, 53
Le Creuset, 19, 21, 48
Cuisinox, 53

Dalisi, Riccardo, 16, 17
Design Council, 11
Design Partners, 42
Dienes, Pieter, 14
Dreyfuss, Henry, 10, 37, 73

Dualit, 32

Ferm, Morgan, 42

gadgets, 35–45
Gaggia, Achille, 16, 57, 61, 73–4
Games, Abram, 63, 74
Gecchelin, Bruno, 44, 74
General Electric, 15
Grange, Kenneth, 11, 31, 74–5
Graves, Michael, 67, 75
Gray, Milner, 11, 51, 75
Greubel, Jürgen, 28
Gropius, Walter, 9, 10
Guild, Lurelle, 19, 19
Guzzini, 35, 44, 71

Habitat, 13–14, 13
Hammarplast, 35, 42
Holland, Nick, 43, 75–6

Industria Produtti Stampati, 33

Kenwood, 11–12, 11, 21, 31
kettles and coffeepots, 16, 57–71
Kissoczy, Maya, 45

Lamble, Kenneth, 51
Loewy, Raymond, 10, 10

machines, 23–33
Magimix, 31, 33
Mellor, David, 13–14, 13
Mies van der Rohe, Ludwig, 10–11
Minuti, Furio, 71
Muller, Gerd Alfred, 30

New-Maid, 64

Nurmesniemi, Antti, 64, 76

Palsby, Ole, 69
La Pavoni, 57, 63
Ponti, Gio, 16
pots and pans, 19–20, 47–55
Powell, Dick, 78
Powell, Seymour, 54
Pyrex, 20, 21

Rams, Dieter, 12, 76–7
Rossi, Aldo, 16, 68, 77
Russell, Gordon, 11
Russell Hobbs, 18, 65

Sabatier, 7, 21, 35, 36
Sala, Niki, 20, 52
Sambonet, Roberto, 20, 21, 51, 77
Santais, Edward Loysel de, 16
Sapper, Richard, 15, 55, 66–7, 77–8
Seiffert, Florian, 68
Seymour, Richard, 78
Siemens, 27
Spong, 23, 24
Sunbeam Electric, 30

Thalmann, Julius, 18, 65
Thermos, 59
Thornton, F J & Co, 37
Tupper, Earl, 17–18, 21, 49, 78

utensils, 35–45

Wagenfeld, Wilhelm, 9, 49, 78–9
Welch, Robert, 41, 79
Welden, W Archibald, 20
Wulf, Franz, 70

Zanuso, Marco, 15, 40, 79